Glue your
picture here.

Child of God

To: ______________________________

From: ______________________________

On the occasion of: ______________________________

Date: ______________________________

Copyright © 2021 Concordia Publishing House
3558 S. Jefferson Ave., St. Louis, MO 63118-3968
1-800-325-3040 • cph.org

Manufactured in China/418531/055760

---

3 4 5 6 7 8 9 10 11 12 34 33 32 31 30 29 28 27 26 25

My First Catechism

Written by Gail Pawlitz
Illustrated by Norm Grock

CONCORDIA PUBLISHING HOUSE · SAINT LOUIS

Over and over.

Bit by bit.

Again and again.

My mother helped me learn memory work in the kitchen. Propped in the windowsill above the sink was the passage for the week. She washed. I dried. She read. I repeated. And there at my mother's side over and over, bit by bit, again and again, I learned God's timeless truths that still guide and comfort me.

This book helps you introduce a young child to God's timeless truths. Bit by bit, you can do what my mother did. And as you do, consider the way young children learn.

Children have short attention spans, so adjust how much you read to their capacity. Introduce one part of the catechism at a time. Say and repeat God's truths. Explain the difficult words. Wonder about the symbols through activities and conversation. Review how God's truths guide daily life. Point at the pictures in this book and talk about how these truths might look in the life of your young child. Explore the entire book in small chunks for big results.

Play is the chief way children learn—through manipulating blocks and dolls, through conversations during dress-up fun or riding on tricycles. Children use conversation to puzzle through and assimilate the big ideas of life. Reading this book can explain those big ideas. They show up in self-talk and role-play.

As God's child, too, you live out your vocation of loving and serving others in God's kingdom. It's a big task with eternal merits. But you needn't worry. Through His Word and in His Sacraments, God is with you! Amen.

CONTENTS

The Ten Commandments

THE FIRST COMMANDMENT

You shall have no other gods.

THE SECOND COMMANDMENT

You shall not misuse the name of the LORD your God.

THE THIRD COMMANDMENT

Remember the Sabbath day by keeping it holy.

THE FOURTH COMMANDMENT

Honor your father and your mother.

THE FIFTH COMMANDMENT

You shall not murder.

THE SIXTH COMMANDMENT

You shall not commit adultery.

THE SEVENTH COMMANDMENT

You shall not steal.

THE EIGHTH COMMANDMENT

You shall not give false testimony against your neighbor.

THE NINTH COMMANDMENT

You shall not covet your neighbor's house.

THE TENTH COMMANDMENT

You shall not covet your neighbor's wife,
or his manservant or maidservant, his ox or donkey,
or anything that belongs to your neighbor.

This symbol helps us think about the Ten Commandments.

Find the two stone tablets. The letters on them are called roman numerals. They are symbols for the Commandments that God wrote on stone tablets. Touch each roman numeral and count. God gave His people Ten Commandments. They tell us how to love Him and others.

Find the mountain. God gave the Commandments to Moses. Then Moses told the Commandments to God's people, young and old, big and small.

Trace the cross. Jesus kept God's Ten Commandments for you and for me.

Make a book with your hands. In the Bible, we can read God's Commandments.

Now, touch your heart. God's Ten Commandments are good. They help us know how to love Him and others. They also help us know when we sin. And that is good too.

Living as God's Child

THINKING, SAYING, AND DOING

Search the pictures. Find someone going to church to hear God's Word. (Third Commandment)

Find someone who did not show love. (Fifth Commandment)

Find someone who is willing to obey. (Fourth Commandment)

EXTRA: Give each other a high five and say, "I'm God's child. His Commandments help me to love and serve others."

The Creed

I believe in God, the Father Almighty, Maker of heaven and earth.

And in Jesus Christ, His only Son, our Lord, who was conceived by the Holy Spirit, born of the Virgin Mary, suffered under Pontius Pilate, was crucified, died and was buried. He descended into hell. The third day He rose again from the dead. He ascended into heaven and sits at the right hand of God, the Father Almighty. From thence He will come to judge the living and the dead.

I believe in the Holy Spirit, the holy Christian church, the communion of saints, the forgiveness of sins, the resurrection of the body, and the life ever-lasting. Amen.

This symbol helps us think about the Apostles' Creed.

Trace the triangle. It has three sides. In this creed, we say what we believe about God—Father, Son, and Holy Spirit. He is three persons yet one God.

Look for the hand. The hand is a symbol for God the Father, who lovingly created all things. God loves and cares for us too.

Find the lamb. Jesus is the Lamb of God. He died for our sins. He rose again on Easter. Jesus won a victory over sin, death, and the devil.

Trace the dove. It is a symbol for the Holy Spirit. The Holy Spirit works through God's Word and the Sacraments. He makes us children of God and keeps us in the faith.

Make a book with your hands. In the Bible, we learn about our God—Father, Son, and Holy Spirit.

Now, touch your heart. When we say the Apostles' Creed, we confess what we believe about God.

Living as God's Child

THINKING, SAYING, AND DOING

Search the pictures.

Find the girl taking care of a cat. God is the Creator of all things. In thanks to God, we serve and obey Him. How do we do that?

Find the girl making a cross. Jesus is our Savior. Make your own cross.

Find the two girls singing about Jesus. The Holy Spirit brings us to faith in Jesus as our Savior. Sing a song about Jesus.

EXTRA: Get out some play dough. Use your hands to form things God created.

The Lord's Prayer

Our Father who art in heaven, hallowed be Thy name, Thy kingdom come, Thy will be done on earth as it is in heaven. Give us this day our daily bread; and forgive us our trespasses as we forgive those who trespass against us; and lead us not into temptation, but deliver us from evil. For Thine is the kingdom and the power and the glory forever and ever. Amen.

This symbol helps us think about the Lord's Prayer.

Look for the big hand. This hand is a symbol for God the Father. He invites us to pray to Him just like dear children talk to their dear father. We can pray anytime and anywhere.

Find the small hands. Fold your small hands. Praying is talking to God. We can pray when we are afraid or sick, sad or happy. We can pray for ourselves or others. We can tell Jesus we are sorry when we sin.

Make a book with your hands. In the Bible, we read that Jesus taught His disciples how to pray. Who taught you to pray?

Now, touch your heart. When we pray the Lord's Prayer, God promises to hear and answer in the best way. Thank You, God!

Living as God's Child

THINKING, SAYING, AND DOING

Search the pictures.

Find the boy who is praying during a storm. God invites us to pray when we are afraid. He will hear us.

Find the girls who are fighting. God says we can ask Him to forgive our sins. He also tells us to forgive others.

Find the boy who is about to eat. He is thanking God for his food. We can do that too. Our daily food is a gift from God.

EXTRA: Take turns praising God for something. Then together, clap your hands.

The Sacrament of Holy Baptism

Baptism is not just plain water, but it is the water included in God's command and combined with God's word. It works forgiveness of sins, rescues from death and the devil, and gives eternal salvation to all who believe this, as the words and promises of God declare.

"Go therefore and make disciples of all nations, baptizing them in the name of the Father and of the Son and of the Holy Spirit, teaching them to observe all that I have commanded you." (Matthew 28:19–20)

This symbol helps us think about Holy Baptism.

Look for the piece of furniture. It is called a font. It holds water for baptizing. In Baptism, God makes us His children through water and His Word.

Find the shell. It is a symbol for Baptism. Cup your hand like a shell.

Count the three drops of water. We are baptized in the name of the Father and of the Son and of the Holy Spirit.

Trace the cross. In Baptism, God gives us the forgiveness of sins, rescues us from evil, and gives us eternal life. Because of Jesus, all this is true. The words and promises of God say so.

Make a book with your hands. In the Bible, we read that Jesus said, "Whoever believes and is baptized will be saved" (Mark 16:16).

Now, touch your heart. Then, clap your hands. Rejoice! Each day is a new day to live as God's child. That's good news.

Living as God's Child

THINKING, SAYING, AND DOING

Search the pictures.

Find the child who is making the sign of the cross. You can make it too. Try it. Remember that you are God's child.

Find the people in a row. Everyone who is baptized belongs to God's big family. Name some people you know in God's family.

Find the Baptism birthday candle. You can celebrate your Baptism birthday.

EXTRA: Look at a baptismal gown or certificate or at photos from a Baptism.

Confession

Confession has two parts.

First, that we confess our sins, and second, that we receive absolution, that is, forgiveness, from the pastor as from God Himself, not doubting, but firmly believing that by it our sins are forgiven before God in heaven.

This symbol helps us think about Confession.

Look for the big person. He is saying, "I'm sorry." You can tell Jesus and others that you are sorry for what you have done wrong.

Find a hand. This hand reminds us that God forgives our sin.

Touch the cross. In church, we confess our sins. Then, we hear the pastor say that God forgives our sins for Jesus' sake.

Make a book with your hands. In the Bible, we read, "Confess your sins to one another" (James 5:16). You can tell others and Jesus that you are sorry for your sins.

Now, touch your heart and ears. When we hear that God forgives our sin, we hear the Absolution. That's a big word with great power—God's power. It means God has forgiven our sin. That is good news.

Living as God's Child

Confession has two parts.

I say,
"I am sorry.
Please
forgive me."

The pastor
says,
"I am God's
servant.
I tell you God
forgives you."

THINKING, SAYING, AND DOING

Look! The heart is broken. What sad thing happened?

Where do you see a cross? Remember that because of Jesus, God is always ready to listen to our confession and forgive His children.

EXTRA: Teach kids to say, "I'm sorry. Please forgive me." Teach them to respond to others by saying, "I forgive you."

The Sacrament of the Altar

This is the true body and blood of our Lord Jesus Christ under the bread and wine, instituted by Christ Himself for us Christians to eat and to drink.

The holy Evangelists Matthew, Mark, Luke, and St. Paul write:

Our Lord Jesus Christ, on the night when He was betrayed, took bread, and when He had given thanks, He broke it and gave it to the disciples and said: "Take, eat; this is My body, which is given for you. This do in remembrance of Me."

In the same way also He took the cup after supper, and when He had given thanks, He gave it to them, saying, "Drink of it, all of you; this cup is the new testament in My blood, which is shed for you for the forgiveness of sins. This do, as often as you drink it, in remembrance of Me."

This sacrament is also called the Lord's Supper, the Lord's Table, Holy Communion, the Breaking of Bread, and the Eucharist.

This symbol helps us think about the Lord's Supper.

Trace the cross. Jesus was the first one to celebrate this special meal. Now God's people celebrate it in church.

Hold up two fingers. In this meal, believers receive the body and blood of Jesus under the bread and wine. Two things you see. Two things you believe.

Find the big cup called a chalice. The cup holds wine. Wine is made from grapes. Bread-like wafers are made from grain. A plate called the paten holds the wafers.

Make a book with your hands. In the Bible, we read about the big gifts we receive in Holy Communion—forgiveness, life, and salvation. Give a big cheer for these gifts.

Now, touch your heart and then your lips. God's people come to the altar to receive God's love and forgiveness. They leave forgiven, thankful, and joyful. Sing a joyful song about Jesus.

Living as God's Child

The Wafer, Christ's Body

The Cup, Christ's Blood

The Altar, the Table of the Lord

THINKING, SAYING, AND DOING

Search the pictures. Find the altar. God's people come to the altar for the Lord's Supper. Children can receive a blessing there. Do you?

Find the cup. The cup holds the wine. Find the wafer.

Touch all the crosses you see. Remember, in this meal, God also gives gifts you can't see. He gives the forgiveness of sins and life forever with Jesus.

EXTRA: Talk about what you see at the Lord's Supper.

The Table of Duties

At church, I hear God's word of love for me. From there, I go and show God's love to others.

In my school and neighborhood, I follow the rules. I play nicely. I show God's love to others.

At home, I eat and play nicely. I pray and rest. I help and obey my parents. I show God's love to others.

THINKING, SAYING, AND DOING

Tell how you like to help at church.
How do you play nicely?
How do you help at home?
What rules do you follow?

What Is Worship?

Worship is God at work. He gives us His gifts, and we respond.

In the church service, God speaks to us through His Word. He comes through the Lord's Supper. He comes in Holy Baptism. You can't see how it happens, but you can believe it.

In the church service, we tell God we are sorry for our sins. We give thanks and pray. We bring our offering. We sing and praise God.

The Church Year

Colors help us tell a story.

Advent Blue

Lenten Violet

Advent Blue says, "For four weeks prepare and sing. Get ready for the coming King."

Christmas White says, "Christ is born. Jump for joy! Celebrate this baby boy."

Epiphany Green says, "Jesus grew. He preached and healed. See Jesus as God's Son revealed."

Lenten Violet says, "Wait and pray. Ask for forgiveness every day."

Palm Sunday Scarlet says, "Let's sing! Hosannas to our Savior King!"

Good Friday Black says, "Jesus died on Calvary. He won eternal life for me."

Easter White says, "The grave is empty. Come and see. Jesus lives! He set us free."

Pentecost Red says, "Tell the news that Jesus saves. Confess, believe, and offer praise."

Christmas White

Palm Sunday Scarlet

Epiphany Green

Easter White

Luther's Seal

TOUCH AND WONDER

This symbol tells a story. Touch and wonder. Find out what it says.

Touch the cross. I wonder about the cross. Why is it black? Think of sin as black.

Touch the heart. I wonder about the heart. Why is it red? It is red for love. God loves us. He sent His Son, Jesus, to die on the cross and rise again to get rid of sin.

Touch the flower. I wonder about the flower. Why is it white? Think of white as pure and holy. The Holy Spirit gives us faith and makes us pure in God's eyes.

Touch something blue. I wonder about the blue. Blue is a happy color. God gives us joy as we believe and trust in Him.

Touch the ring. I wonder about the ring. Why is it gold? Gold is precious. Think of heaven. It is God's precious home for His children.

The black cross, red heart, white flower, blue sky, and gold ring tell a story. When you see Luther's Seal, you can tell others the story too!

Prayers

Luther's Morning Prayer

I thank You, my heavenly Father, through Jesus Christ, Your dear Son, that You have kept me this night from all harm and danger; and I pray that You would keep me this day also from sin and every evil, that all my doings and life may please You. For into Your hands I commend myself, my body and soul, and all things. Let Your holy angel be with me, that the evil foe may have no power over me. Amen.

Luther's Evening Prayer

I thank You, my heavenly Father, through Jesus Christ, Your dear Son, that You have graciously kept me this day; and I pray that You would forgive me all my sins where I have done wrong, and graciously keep me this night. For into Your hands I commend myself, my body and soul, and all things. Let Your holy angel be with me, that the evil foe may have no power over me. Amen.

Lord God, heavenly Father, bless us and these Your gifts which we receive from Your bountiful goodness, through Jesus Christ, our Lord. Amen.

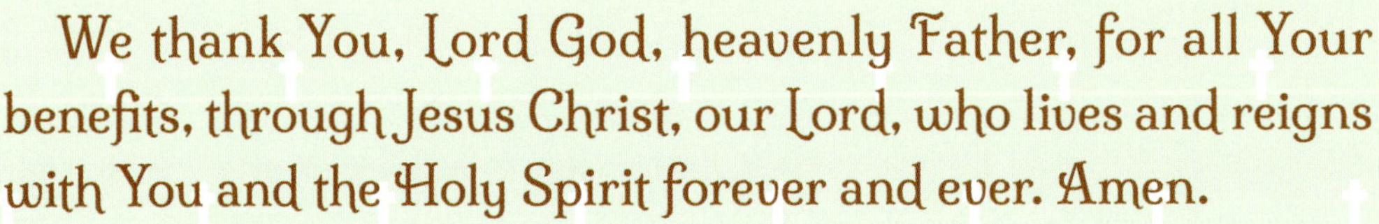

We thank You, Lord God, heavenly Father, for all Your benefits, through Jesus Christ, our Lord, who lives and reigns with You and the Holy Spirit forever and ever. Amen.

Be our light in the darkness, O Lord, and in Your great mercy defend us from all perils and dangers of this night; for the love of Your only Son, Jesus Christ, our Lord. Amen. (*LSB*, p. 257)

I am trusting Thee, Lord Jesus, trusting only Thee;
Trusting Thee for full salvation, great and free.
I am trusting Thee to guide me; Thou alone shalt lead,
Ev'ry day and hour supplying all my need. Amen. (*LSB* 729)

Heavenly Father, You made such a wonderful world, and You made me too. Thank You for sending Your own Son, Jesus, to save me. Amen. (*GIF*, p. 7)

Lord God, thank You for watching over us and providing everything we need. Remind me to pray to You, because You promise to answer all my prayers for Jesus' sake. Amen. (*GIF*, p. 59)